Why we celebrate

HALLOWEEN: A SHORT HISTORY

seeking the hidden roots and symbols of a Celtic harvest festival in the modern day fun

Copyright © 2019 by Home Hearth Press

All rights reserved. No part of this publication may be reproduced, distributed, or transmitted in any form or by any means, including photocopying, recording, or other electronic or mechanical methods, without the prior written permission of the publisher, except in the case of brief quotations embodied in critical reviews and certain other noncommercial uses permitted by copyright law.

For permission requests, write to the publisher, addressed "Attention: Permissions Coordinator," at: thescienecewomen@gmail.com

Introduction

It's easy to dismiss Halloween as a ploy to sell more candy.

The holiday, however, is steeped in ancient symbolism and carries a deeper meaning about the rhythm of the seasons and our eternal connection to the earth.

Understanding the roots of the holiday, which began as a harvest festival, helps make it a more meaningful celebration than simply the exchange of candy.

Halloween is a complex, multi-layered celebration with lots of influences and traditions. It marks a time of transition between seasons - the end of summer and the beginning of the dark days of winter. This ancient celebration was a way for people to understand nature and to try to influence and control it.

This book aims to present the history of Halloween in clear, simplified terms, so that kids, and families, can begin to appreciate the rich symbolism and ancient customs of the holiday.

As modern society becomes more estranged from food production and nature, the traditions that formed Halloween remind us that we are intricately connected to the land, the food it produces, and the changing seasons.

Beginnings of the Halloween celebration: Celtic and Roman

The celebration we now know as Halloween has its roots deep in time.

A lot of Halloween customs and traditions we celebrate can be traced back to an ancient Celtic harvest festival called Samhain, celebrated on October 31.

The name Samhain means "summer's end".

Some traditions probably also came from Roman beliefs and celebrations, such as Pomona - the goddess of fruit, seeds, and abundance, and Parentalia - a festival of the dead.

Why end of October was a special time

The end of October was a special time for the ancient Celts.

It was a time of transition between seasons. It marked the end of summer and the beginning of the long, dark days of the winter months.

For the ancient Celts the end of October was a time of rest after the harvest. A time for shepherds to come home with their flocks. A time for tribal gatherings, marriage and end of warfare. It was a time to focus on family and home.

What the Samhain feast celebrated

The Samhain festival celebrated the end of harvest season and praised the bounty of the land. It helped people prepared for the end of summer and the coming long, dark days of winter.

People gave thanks to the supernatural powers they believed controlled the cycle of nature.

During winter no food could be grown, so people were dependent on the food they produced during the summer and harvested in fall to get them through the long winter months.

The Samhain festival was a way to celebrate the power of nature and to perform rituals that people believed would help them, and their livestock, survive the winter.

This transition between seasons, the transition from long, sunny days with abundant food, to short dark ones, with scarce food supplies, also took on a supernatural meaning.

The Dark Side of Celebration

The ancient Celts believed that the time of the Samhain festival was a liminal time. It was a time when the separation between this world and the world of fairies and spirits melted away, and all sorts of ghosts, demons and witches slipped from their world into this world.

Samhain was a night when mischievous spirits roamed about freely, played pranks in the homes, stole food, and caused harm to livestock.

How to get rid of mischievous spirits

The ancient Celts tried different ways to scare away spirits. They used fire, such as bonfires and torches, and dressed in masks and costumes to keep ghosts, witches and demons away from their homes and livestock.

They also prepared food to feed the spirits in order to get on their good side. They left food offerings outside houses and set feast tables piled high with fruits and crops.

At the end of the Samhain feast, masked and costumed people danced through the village to lead the spirits away for good and ensure a peaceful winter.

Over time, these rituals developed into customs and traditions that were performed each October 31 and become part of the folklore of Halloween.

The lands of the ancient Celts became part of Britain, Ireland and Scotland, and the Samhain celebration became incorporated into their customs.

How Halloween Came to Us

The Celtic traditions of Samhain were performed each October 31, season after season through the centuries.

On Halloween night children went caroling from house to house, wearing costumes, carrying lamps made out of carved turnips, and collected candy.

In North America, to begin with, Halloween was only celebrated by some Irish settlers. But as more Irish immigrants arrived, the idea caught on and the celebration became popular in the beginning of the 20th century.

There are several explanations for the tradition of carving and carrying Jack-O-Lanterns.

Why Jack-O-Lanterns?

In keeping with the ancient Celtic tradition, in Britain, Ireland and Scotland, carved Jack-O-Lanterns lit by candles were carried by carolers on Halloween to frighten away mischievous spirits from homes. Instead of the pumpkins used today, Jack-O-Lanterns were traditionally carved out of turnips, which were native to Britain, Ireland and Scotland.

Only when the custom moved to North America, where pumpkins were abundant during October, did the pumpkin become the Jack-O-Lantern gourd of choice.

Another explanation could be based on witch lore. People believed that witches used skulls with a candle inside to light the way to their secret meetings. Carved pumpkins were made to look like those eerie skulls.

Costumes and masks

Just like during the ancient Celtic Samhain feast, modern Halloween is a night when mischievous spirits roam freely and play tricks on people. To scare away ghosts and other spirits, people wear masks and dress in costumes.

Since ancient times, people have been dressing up as the beings they are trying to scare away. They took ideas for their costumes and masks from the folklore descriptions of these beings. Today we dress up as what we imagine witches, demons, ghosts and zombies look like.

Trick or Treat and Candy

Feeding the mischievous spirits was an important part of the ancient Samhain festival. Treats were offered to the ghosts, witches and demons to keep them from playing tricks.

Traditionally, offerings were made of food people collected in the fall - fruits, such as apples and nuts, such as hazelnuts and acorns. This tradition has evolved over time and today we offer each other candy on Halloween night.

From costumes and masks, to Jack-O-Lanterns and treats, it's surprising to learn that so many of the Halloween traditions we do on October 31 came to us from an ancient Celtic fall festival celebrating the harvest season and the bounty of the land.

Learning about the history of Halloween helps us understand why we go from house to house, dressed in costumes, to collect candy.

And now you can tell your friends about it.

Things to Talk About

1. The Samhain festival celebrated the changing of the seasons, the cycle of nature, and the food produced by the land. Why is the changing of the seasons and the cycle of nature so important to people? What is significant about each season? Do we have other holidays that celebrate the different seasonal changes?

2. Some of the fruits and nuts used traditionally in the Samhain feast took on supernatural meanings. The hazelnut was considered a god by the Celts. Research other sacred foods that were used in seasonal celebrations by the Celts and other societies and cultures.

3. Fall harvest feasts, and some of the Halloween traditions we still see today, go back to ancient Rome. Making cider from freshly picked apples, for example, and bobbing for apples were part of the celebration of the fruit goddess Pomona. Research other ancient Roman traditions we still celebrate today. How do ancient traditions influence modern ones and how do customs change over time?

4. The ancient traditions that became part of Halloween were very different from the modern celebration. Are there ways to make Halloween more meaningful for your family? What are some ways to bring back traditional fall feast customs to help feel more connected to nature and its bounty?

5. Look up unknown terms used in this book, such as: liminal or folklore.